WHAT PARENTS SAY ABOUT THIS BOOK:

"You've put together a most helpful and wonderful publication..."
— *E.J., Bodega, California*

"I found the book to be well developed and it lends itself to easy discussion between children and parents."
— *J.F., Clovis, New Mexico*

"The book is very informative and just right for my 9 and 12 year olds."
— *M.C., Stedman, North Carolina*

"It's a great book — it made talking about sex with my daughter a positive experience and helped me feel comfortable and cover all the topics and moral issues."
— *E.M., Newington, Connecticut*

"It's the best book I've found for my 9-year old son."
— *S.U., Middletown, Connecticut*

"My husband and I are very impressed with both the information in the book and its presentation."
— *P.K., Newington, Connecticut*

LET'S TALK ABOUT...s-e-x

a read-and-discuss guide for people 9 to 12 and their parents

by Sam Gitchel and Lorri Foster

Revised Edition 1995

PLANNED PARENTHOOD OF CENTRAL CALIFORNIA
255 North Fulton / Fresno, CA 93701 / (209) 488-4917

Revised edition, 1995
Copyright © 1982, 1983, 1986 and 1995 by Planned Parenthood of Central California

Printed in the United States of America

Illustrations: Andrea Cooper

Cover design: Waverly Boling

ISBN: 0-9610122-2-6

Also available in Spanish, "Hablemos Acerca Del...S-e-x-o"

*Quantity Purchases: Agencies and organizations may qualify for special
discounts on quantity orders of these titles. For information write:*
Planned Parenthood of Central California
Publications Department
255 N. Fulton
Fresno, CA 93701
or call (209) 488-4917

CONTENTS

THIS PART IS FOR PARENTS

A WORD TO PARENTS ABOUT THIS BOOK

This book can help you and your son or daughter talk more comfortably about sex. The first part is for you, the parent. It will help you get ready to talk with your child about the information in the rest of the book. The second part is for your preadolescent girl or boy to read and discuss with you. It gives factual information about growing up. Perhaps more important, it also includes activities which will help you discuss your family values and beliefs. Your children need to understand your values, and you are the best person to explain what you believe. Working together on the activities can open the door to more honest communication as they enter their teenage years.

******

WHY PARENTS NEED TO TALK

Our children learn about sex every day. Television, bathroom walls, billboards, playground jokes, and popular music all give them messages about sex. Unfortunately, most of these messages are not very helpful. They usually don't explain basic facts. They almost never show the responsibilities that go along with sex, and may lead children to think that sex is a carefree game.

Sometimes school programs can help. A few schools do offer complete sex education courses. These programs not only provide important factual information; they also help students learn to understand themselves and make responsible decisions. Most schools, though, provide only two or three lectures which cover some basic facts about reproduction and sexually transmitted infections. While this information is valuable, many students' questions remain unanswered. Even if your child is lucky enough to have a good school sex education program, nothing can replace the kind of teaching parents can do. As a parent you can give your child information in a personal way and at times that best meet his or her needs. And no school program can teach your family values, the particular beliefs that you want to pass along to your child.

Of course, children have already learned a great deal from their everyday experiences as part of their family and community. From the way they are fed, held, and comforted as infants, they learn about closeness and physical affection. From relationships with family and friends, they learn about caring and responsibility. From their parents' way of handling their squabbles with other toddlers, they learn about sharing and consideration for others. From

listening to the way parents talk with each other and other family members, children learn about love, communication, and getting along in a close relationship. All these experiences, and many others, will influence their attitudes, feelings, and behavior, now and in the future.

Even though so much learning takes place without words, it is still important for families to talk about sex. A child who has correct information and a clear sense of family values is more likely to make careful decisions. Parents need to show that they are willing to talk, rather than waiting for their children to come to them with questions. Avoiding the subject may suggest that sex is too difficult, too embarrassing, or perhaps too dirty to be talked about. This makes it even harder for children to ask for the information they need. They may be left with only the hodgepodge of ideas they pick up outside the family.

A GOOD TIME TO TALK

A very good time to build family communication about sex is when your child is between 9 and 12 years old. At this age most children are very interested in trying to understand how everything works, including their own bodies. Yet they are still young enough to talk about sex and reproduction without too much embarrassment. They often try to figure out sex and reproduction in the same matter-of-fact way they might try to understand how an automobile engine works.

As their own bodies, or their friends' bodies, begin changing, preteens become very interested in what is normal. Since some begin to develop early and others lag behind, many youngsters are very concerned about being different from their friends. Talking with parents can help to reassure them that these differences are completely normal.

This is also an excellent time for parents to begin discussing their values and beliefs about issues such as dating rules, "dirty" jokes, sex before marriage, etc. Few preteens are ready to carry on long discussions on such topics. But they are likely to remember what you say if you keep your remarks simple, specific, and do not insist that they immediately agree.

As youngsters become teenagers, talking about sex usually becomes more difficult. It is normal for teenagers to want more independence and some distance from their own families. They need a reasonable amount of privacy and trust. Also, as their sexual feelings become stronger, they may be less able to discuss sex in the straightforward way of the preadolescent. But if you have already established a pattern of honestly talking about sex-related topics, it is more likely that you will be able to continue this communication through adolescence.

HOW MUCH DOES YOUR CHILD NEED TO KNOW?

Like most other parents, you may wonder what topics you need to discuss with your preteen child. The following checklist includes the basic topics that all children, both boys and girls, need to know about in order to understand the changes of puberty. These are explained in detail later in this book.

It is not easy for most parents to talk about sex. But discussing these topics frankly at the right times can help your child to grow up with more confidence and less worry about normal feelings. Your willingness to talk openly about these subjects will make it easier for your child to come to you as the teen years bring new interests and concerns.

MALE & FEMALE BODIES
_____ Male sexual and reproductive organs, internal and external
_____ Female sexual and reproductive organs, internal and external
_____ Physical changes of puberty, male and female
_____ How these changes relate to reproduction
_____ That these changes bring about new feelings and emotions
_____ That people mature at different rates

MENSTRUATION
_____ What it is
_____ When it occurs
_____ That it is normal
_____ How to be prepared

ERECTIONS & WET DREAMS
_____ What they are
_____ That they are normal

MASTURBATION
_____ What it is
_____ That it is not harmful
_____ That it is normal to do it or not to do it
_____ Your family standards about it

SEXUAL INTERCOURSE

_____ What it is

_____ How it is related to pregnancy

_____ Your beliefs about how it relates
to love, marriage, birth control, etc.

RISKS

_____ Sexually transmitted infections

_____ Unintended pregnancy

_____ Hurt feelings

_____ Relationship problems

Are there other things **you** consider important, which are not included in this checklist, but which you want to be sure your child understands? The spaces below are left for you to add these topics:

_____

_____

_____

_____

SOME SUGGESTIONS

I. BUILDING SELF-ESTEEM

This is probably the most important influence on your children's sexual adjustment. As they become teenagers your children will be faced with many difficult and important decisions. People who feel good about themselves are less likely to let others pressure them into making unwise choices, and don't need to use others to make themselves look good or feel good. They are more likely to make responsible decisions about sex, and about many other things as well. Here are some things you can do to help your children feel good about themselves:

Let them know that you appreciate them. Recognize their talents, personality, looks, accomplishments and anything else you can think of. Avoid comparing them with others. Help them discover their own special strengths.

Treat them with respect. Ask for their opinions. Listen to their ideas and feelings. Think about what they say to you. Their self-respect begins with the respect and consideration they receive from you and others.

Don't expect too much or too little. Many youngsters feel insulted because they think their parents treat them like little kids. Others get discouraged because they feel their parents expect more than they can do. It is important to let them know that you have confidence in them. You can support them without pushing, and protect them without keeping them from new experiences.

Avoid too much criticism. Teens are extremely sensitive to criticism. If they hear too many negatives they may just stop listening. They often do want to hear parents' opinions, when expressed tactfully and with love. And when your children fail at something or make a mistake, let them know that it is not the end of the world.

II. FEELING UNCOMFORTABLE

All parents feel at least a little uncomfortable talking to their children about sex. Maybe your parents never talked with you about sex, and so you feel unsure about what to say. Maybe you are worried that you don't know the answers to all the questions that might come up. Nobody does. Feeling uncomfortable doesn't have to stop you from talking. There are some things you can do to help feel more at ease, though.

First, look through the second part of this book. You will then be familiar with what your child will be reading. You will notice that there are several places where it says "Ask your mom or dad about...". Think about what you will say when your child asks you. Maybe you will want to discuss your answers ahead of time with your spouse, a close friend, or a relative. If you want to read more about certain topics, you could try some of the readings listed at the back of this book.

Just the idea of saying some of the words in this book, words like "penis" or "vagina," may make you feel uncomfortable. You might want to practice saying them to yourself, possibly in front of a mirror, before you try talking with your child. You may feel a little silly at first, but with practice this feeling will wear off. If you do feel embarrassed when you try to talk, you can admit this honestly to your son or daughter. Almost everyone feels that sex is a special, private subject. Admitting your own discomfort will probably help you both feel more comfortable.

Finally, you don't have to do this all alone. You can certainly include your spouse or another trusted adult. There will be times when both adults together can be involved in talking, or each can talk to the child separately.

Many parents wonder if it is okay for a mother to talk with her son about sex or for a father to talk with his daughter. The answer is **yes!** In fact, sometimes talking with a parent of the opposite sex has special advantages. Most preteenagers and early teenagers are very interested in how other people see them, especially people of the other sex. The opposite-sex parent can give this viewpoint. For example, a mother can help her son understand how women think and feel about men. She can help him to understand and respect girls' thoughts and feelings. After all, she was once a girl herself!

Mothers are usually more willing than fathers to discuss sex with either boys or girls, but fathers also have a lot to offer children of both sexes. A parent's willingness to talk **and** to listen are much more important than which sex the parent happens to be.

III. LISTENING IS IMPORTANT TOO

To **talk** to your children in a way that will really help, you have to also **listen** to their words, and to the feelings behind their words. You must try to see things through their eyes. If they feel that you understand them, they are much more likely to talk openly with you. One of the best ways to see the world through your child's eyes is to try to remember yourself at the same age. Spend a few minutes thinking about these questions:

> When did you notice your body starting to change, and how did you feel about it?
> What ideas did you have that were mistaken?
> What did your parents tell you about sex? At what age?
> What did they say that was helpful? What was not helpful?
> What do you wish they had said or done to help you understand yourself and others?
> What do you want to do in the same way with your children?
> What do you want to do differently?

Some of the things your children go through will be similar to things you experienced when you were young. Others will not be. It may help to relate a few of your own experiences. The danger is in going too far, saying "I know exactly what you're going through" about everything. Young people are quickly turned off by this approach. Careful listening also makes it easier for you, because you will have a better idea about exactly what your child needs to know. Before answering a difficult question, it may help to ask your child what he or she thinks the answer is. The reply may tell you what you need to say next.

For example, a preadolescent might ask: "Why do people have sex?" (Books could be written about this subject.) What does she mean when she says "sex"? Kissing? Petting? Sexual intercourse? And even after you find out what she means by "sex," there is more than one answer—people have sex for a number of reasons. Probably this preadolescent heard or saw something specific that triggered her question. You might say:

> "There can be different reasons. Why do you think people have sex?"
> "I don't know...(silence)...well—Suzanne said people have sex when they love each other."
> "What do you suppose she means...'having sex'?"
> "I don't know...I guess kissing and stuff."
> "Yeah...anything else?"
> "Well...she said something like...'inner'...uh...'innercourse,' I think."
> "She was probably talking about sexual intercourse—"
> "Yeah, that's it..."

"We sometimes call it 'making love.' That's because when a man and a woman love each other, they like to get as close together as possible. They may decide to have sexual intercourse. The man's penis fits inside the woman's vagina, and — "

"Oh, yuck. . . why would they want to do that?"

"It may sound strange to you now, but at the right time it can be a really nice way of showing love, and it feels good to both people. You will understand those feelings better when you're older."

"How old do you have to be?"

"Well, people have different ideas on that. Your mom and I believe it's best to wait until you're married. For one thing, when people have intercourse, the woman could get pregnant. . . ."

By gently asking a few questions, this father was able to talk with his daughter about the things she really wanted to know. A hasty, preachy answer might have cut off the conversation. But he showed that he was willing to talk **and listen,** so his daughter asked more questions.

Of course there is more to be discussed eventually. All the important things cannot be covered in one sitting. And some things will probably need to be brought up more than once. There is no need to sit down and have a BIG SERIOUS TALK. The best way to talk about sex is in the everyday conversations which are a natural part of family life.

IV. FACTS AND VALUES

Your child needs to know both the **facts** about sex and your family **values.** Facts are facts. They are the same for everyone, whether we like them or not. Values are different for different people. Our decisions about what we like or dislike, what we approve or disapprove, are based on our individual values. For instance, it is a fact that a lot of unmarried people are having sex these days. We may or may not think it's right, according to our values. But it is still a fact.

Preteens will soon be facing important decisions about sex. To handle these well, they need to be able to recognize the difference between facts and value judgements. The best way we can help them is by making this difference clear in the things we say every day.

For practice, try deciding whether each of these statements is a value statement or a statement of fact. (Hint: value statements often include one of these words: should, ought, good, bad, right, wrong.)

"By the time they are 13, girls should get more interested in being pretty and ladylike."
Value judgement

"By the time they are 13, a lot of girls get more interested in being pretty and ladylike."
Fact

"A guy who has not started dating by the time he is 17 must be weird."
Value judgement

"Most people masturbate at some time during their lives."
Fact

"Nowadays, many people think it's okay to have intercourse before marriage."
Fact

"It's okay to have sex before marriage, if both people know what they are doing."
Value judgement

"When it comes to premarital sex, it is worse for girls to do it than for guys."
Value judgement. (While it's a fact that only girls get pregnant, the word "worse" adds a judgement.)

"Many girls who have a baby while in high school never get a diploma."
Fact

V. QUESTIONS, QUESTIONS

Preteens probably will not ask direct questions about values. Still they may mention things which give you a chance to discuss your views. For instance, "Janie says when you're 13 you're old enough to go steady." Here is your opportunity to say what you believe about dating, and why you believe it. Your child may or may not agree with what you say right then. But if you can say it respectfully you will keep the door open for continued communication on this subject.

Preteenagers are very curious about their bodies and how they work. They do not always feel free to ask questions, however. Whether they ask or not, here are some of the things they often want to know:

Why can't men have babies?
Does menstruation (or ejaculation, intercourse, childbirth) hurt? Why?
What happens to the sperm cells that don't fertilize the egg?
What about eggs that don't get fertilized?
Why do babies look like their parents?
What causes twins? Siamese twins?
Why do some babies turn out to be boys and others girls?
How does a baby stay alive inside the mother?
What does "making it" (or "getting down," etc.) mean?
What is a wet dream? Do girls have them?
Why are some children adopted?
Do boys have periods? Why not?
When will I develop like my friends?
What does "masturbation" mean?
What's a rubber (condom) for?
Why do kids say dirty words?
What's an abortion?
What are men's balls for?
What is a homosexual?
What is an STI (sexually transmitted infection) or AIDS, herpes, etc.?
How do you catch it?

It is perfectly normal for a preteen child to be interested in these topics. Of course, some parents find that they do not know the answers to all of their child's questions. Many are answered in the second part of this book. Some other good reading is listed at the end. We recommend having a good reference book on sexuality to keep at home. This gives the message that you want your child to get the right information, and that home is a place where questions can be answered.

VI. SEXUAL FEELINGS

Some parents worry that talking about sexuality, and especially admitting that everyone has sexual feelings as they mature, will encourage children to experiment with sex too early. Quite the contrary! In fact, recognizing sexual feelings for what they are can help your soon-to-be-teenager resist being "swept away in the heat of passion." Preteens need to be prepared in advance, so they can tell the difference between sexual feelings, peer pressure, and falling in love. It is much easier to start discussing these topics at this stage, before the moods and conflicts of adolescence begin.

In today's world young people already get plenty of messages telling them that sex feels good, or that it will make them feel like grownup men or women. That is exactly why it is so important that they have parents who are willing to discuss the power of sexual feelings, and the difference between **feeling** and **doing**.

VII. HAZARDS AND RISKS

Sexuality education would not be complete without discussing risks, such as sexually transmitted infections (including AIDS), unintended pregnancy, and emotional upsets. This book begins the process by introducing the basic facts for preadolescents. It is intended to be a start for further learning.

There are several reasons to continue your parent-child discussion of these issues into the teenage years. First, more detailed information will be appropriate for your maturing teenager, after he or she learns the basics. Second, repeated information is more likely to be retained. And, finally, "current" information is continually changing, as new medical findings, tests, and treatments appear every week. Up-to-date pamphlets and videos, available from your county health department or local Planned Parenthood® organization, can be especially valuable in covering these topics (or see the reading list at the end of this book).

Over the next few years, you need to be sure your early teenager is familiar with the following:

How AIDS and other STIs are transmitted Adolescents need to know about the specific sexual activities which can transmit these infections (as well as sharing needles to shoot drugs). These include vaginal, oral, and anal sex. These forms of sexual activity are common among adolescents but often ignored by well-meaning parents who feel uncomfortable discussing them. Keep in mind that the ways STIs are transmitted differ somewhat from one disease to the next. For instance, genital warts and herpes can be transmitted by any genital contact, with or without intercourse.

How STIs (and pregnancy) are prevented The simple answer, "abstinence," is a strong start. Young people certainly need adult support and sound reasons for abstaining from sexual activities. The "read-together" section of this book opens the door for talking about these matters.

Eventually, though, nearly everyone has a sexual relationship and must deal with these risks. For many, sexual experimentation begins in the early teen years. Although your preadolescent may seem young for a discussion of safer sex, the information is more easily and effectively conveyed ahead of time. Your discussion of prevention should include a description of how to obtain and use condoms and spermicides.

Some parents worry that this may encourage sexual activity. However, an early adolescent can easily understand a two-tiered message: *"We've talked about some of the reasons why it's better to wait to have sex. But I want you to know how to protect yourself, even if you don't use the information for quite a while."*

Emotional risks Young people also need to know that sex raises the emotional risks of a relationship. While sex is often portrayed as "casual," few adolescents experience it this way. Adding sex to an immature relationship increases the risk of feeling hurt, jealous, smothered, or used.

As you discuss these risks with your preteen or teenager, aim to keep a sense of balance. All too often, sexuality education has been a lesson in "the terrible things that can happen to you if you do it." Being able to talk about the positive as well as the negative aspects of sexuality will make you a more credible, "askable" parent. For preadolescents, a key message is that they can prevent serious problems by making sensible decisions, and eventually grow up to enjoy healthy, satisfying sexual lives.

One final note. Two groups of young people merit special attention: those who think they may be gay and those who have a family member infected by HIV. Both can benefit from additional support and information, beyond the scope of this book. To find out about counseling or support groups, check with your local AIDS service organization or mental health agency.

VIII. IF THEY DON'T ASK

Because sex is so rarely discussed openly in families, many children learn not to bring up the subject with their own parents. What do you do if your child does not ask? Here are some ideas that have worked for other parents:

Show that it's okay to talk about sexual issues by talking with your spouse or other adults when the children are around. Include teens or preteens in the discussion when appropriate.

Go to one of the movies your children go to, watch one of their TV shows, or listen to their music. This can open the door to discussions of sex and values. If you disapprove of messages you see or hear, tell your children politely what it is about these messages that you don't like.

Comment on sex-related events in everyday life. If your children notice a pregnant friend, or show curiosity about tampons or other personal products, that is a good starting point for talking about reproduction or menstruation.

A few things not to do:

Don't tell them "You're not old enough to know about that." This comment gives the message that you are not willing to discuss this, and perhaps other sensitive subjects. If they are already thinking about any topic, then they need correct information about it, in terms appropriate to their age.

When talking about everyday things, don't make comments that are too harsh or too general. Too many statements like "Look at her—that's disgusting!" can turn off further discussion. It is better to be less negative and more specific: "She is a pretty woman, but I don't think the grocery store is the right place to wear a bikini." This type of statement tells your children more about your values.

Don't tease them about their changing bodies and feelings, and don't allow other family members to tease them either. Such teasing only adds pain at a time when most young-sters are already very sensitive.

Don't use too much humor when you talk about sex. Humor, at the right time, can help to relieve embarrassment. But if most of your talk is in the form of jokes, your children may get the message that sex is not a subject you are willing to talk about seriously.

IX. WHEN *NOT* TO TALK ABOUT SEX

It is better not to talk with your child about sex if the experience is too tense and unpleasant. Do not try to carry on a discussion:

—When your child **strongly** refuses to do so, or appears extremely nervous or sick. You can try again later. (Such an extreme reaction is possibly a sign that your child has been sexually abused. If you suspect that abuse has actually occurred, the way you respond can make a big difference. You might gently assure your child that it is safe to tell you if anything happpened, even if someone has warned "don't tell your parents." Indicate that you believe what your child is saying. Be as calm and matter-of-fact as possible. Reassure your child that you still love her or him as much as before. Finally, find a good counselor for your child to talk with. Your local rape counseling center can suggest qualified professionals.)

—When you are in the middle of a family argument or crisis. The time right after, when things are getting back to normal, may be a much better time.

—When you are **extremely** embarrassed, disgusted, or fearful about sex. You might need to talk first to a close friend or counselor about your feelings.

—When you are experiencing sexual problems in your marriage. Again, it may be better to wait until you have resolved your own problems before talking with your child.

Of course not every question has to be answered immediately. It is certainly okay to wait if, for instance, your child asks about tampons in the grocery checkout line. Or if you just want to take a while to think about your answer. You might say, "Let's talk about that when we get home," or "I'd like to give that a little thought." Then be sure that you do follow up without waiting to be asked again.

WHAT DO YOU HOPE TO ACCOMPLISH?

By using this book you can give your children basic facts about sex which will take away unnecessary fears and worries. By talking together, day by day, you can give them a clearer idea of what your family believes. You may enjoy a greater feeling of trust, because your children will know that you are willing to talk even about difficult subjects.

Do you expect that your children will discuss all their sexual concerns with you? It probably will not happen. No matter how good your relationship is, your teenagers will probably choose to keep some things to themselves, or maybe share them only with their friends. That is a normal part of growing up. But if you have shown that you are willing to talk, **and to listen,** they are more likely to make responsible decisions, and to ask for your advice when they really need it.

In sexual matters, as in everything else, your children will ultimately have to make their own decisions. Naturally you want to help them avoid unwise choices. You also want to help them understand that sex can be a very important and satisfying part of their lives. By making sure that they have correct information, a clear idea of your beliefs, and plenty of chances to communicate with you, you are giving them the best possible start in this direction.

THE REST OF THIS BOOK
IS FOR
CHILDREN AND PARENTS
TO READ TOGETHER

(and talk about together, too . . .)

If you are between 9 and 13 years old, there's something you should know about. It's something called **PUBERTY**. It's not as strange as it sounds, it's not a disease, it's not a tall building that must be leaped at a single bound. And it's definitely **not** a waste of time.

It might be happening right now; if not, it will be starting soon. One day you notice your body is starting to change, and you may think something is going wrong. Especially if no one has told you these changes are **NORMAL.**

That's what this book is for: to let you know what kind of changes to expect.

WHAT IS IT?

Puberty is a few years of your life when your body and your feelings change very quickly. Puberty is a big step toward having the kind of body and feelings you will have as an adult. This period of rapid changing begins any time between the ages of 9 and 16, and lasts for 3 or 4 years.

You will keep changing all through your life -- though probably a little more slowly after puberty. You won't wake up one morning and suddenly be an adult. Becoming an adult happens gradually. Keep reading and you will find out how.

EVERYBODY CHANGES

You've probably noticed that you and your friends are not all changing in the same ways or at the same time. Some kids get a lot taller before the other parts of their bodies catch up. Some get chubby, for a while, before their height catches up.

A girl's breasts and hips grow larger, and so her waist looks smaller. A boy's shoulders grow broader, and he gets more muscles all over. Skin gets more oily, especially on the face. That's why some people get pimples (but keeping extra clean can help). Hair all over the body gets a little darker and coarser. It starts

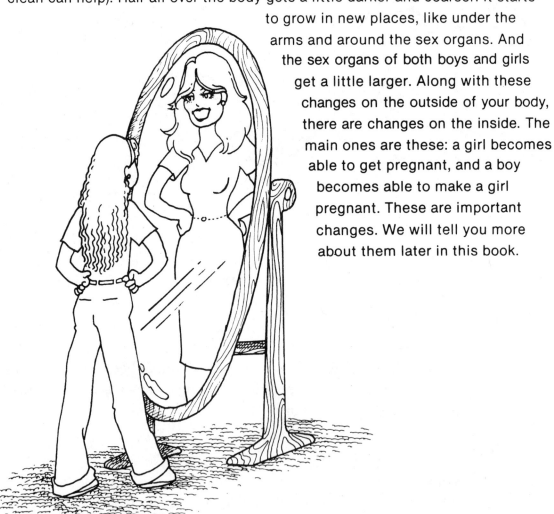

to grow in new places, like under the arms and around the sex organs. And the sex organs of both boys and girls get a little larger. Along with these changes on the outside of your body, there are changes on the inside. The main ones are these: a girl becomes able to get pregnant, and a boy becomes able to make a girl pregnant. These are important changes. We will tell you more about them later in this book.

WHAT IS NORMAL?

A lot of kids worry because they believe
they are changing too soon or too late.
If you're a girl, you may wish your
breasts were larger or smaller. You
may hope you don't start having
periods much sooner or later than
your friends. If you're a boy, you
may wonder about being too tall
or too short, about the size of
your penis, or about hair growing
in places that it never grew before.
Whether you are changing fast
or slow, there's no need to worry.

Most girls begin the changes of puberty a year or two earlier than most boys.
Anyone who starts much earlier than 9 or later than 16 should be checked by a
doctor. The exact time your body will begin making these changes depends
on your parents -- if they started changing at a young age, you probably will,
too. If they started later, that is probably when you will start.

Ask your parents if they can remember when their bodies started changing:

Did they start sooner or later than their friends? _____

At about what age? _____

What body changes did they notice first? _____

_____

How did they feel about these changes?_____

_____

What do they remember most about this time?_____

_____

27

YOUR FEELINGS AND IMAGINATION

Growing up is not just a matter of your body changing. It also has to do with how you feel and the things you do. Most people have strong feelings during puberty: suddenly feeling excited, broken-hearted, loving, hating, angry, sad, happy, scared. . . maybe several different ways at the same time. Moods come and go, and you may not know why. You should know that it is not unusual for this to happen.

And you may think some pretty weird things now and then. . . wonderful things, awful things, some that could never really happen, and some that could. It is normal to imagine all sorts of things, even those you would never actually do. There is nothing wrong with using your imagination.

Daydreaming is one way to learn about yourself and think about how you might handle new situations. And there is nothing wrong with having a lot of different emotions. But if your thoughts or feelings are keeping you unhappy, or taking up so much of your time that you can't do other things, you might want some help. Some good people to talk with are:

—your parents
—a counselor (your parents can probably help you find one)
—your minister, priest or rabbi
—another adult you can trust, such as your favorite teacher
—a local telephone hotline . . . look in the yellow pages of the phone book under "Crisis Intervention"

ACTING OLDER

Growing up also means doing new things. You will soon be old enough to do many things you couldn't do when you were a child. Many teenagers enjoy new experiences like wearing makeup, shaving, learning to drive, wearing "in" clothes, dating (or talking about it), or earning their own spending money. Some even try things that are dangerous and can lead to trouble, like experimenting with sex, alcohol, or drugs.

You will have a lot of decisions to make in the next few years. Many of your friends will begin to do new things, and you will need to decide whether to join in or wait awhile. Your parents can help you figure out when you are old enough for adult activities. Of course there are things which some adults do that your family may disapprove of at **any** age. Figuring out what's right for you will be easier if you know where your parents stand.

Which of the things in this list have you discussed with your parents?

☐ teenagers learning to drive   ☐ boys calling girls on the phone
☐ girls wearing makeup   ☐ girls calling boys on the phone
☐ teenagers dating   ☐ teenagers smoking cigarettes
☐ teenagers earning spending money ☐ teenagers trying drugs and alcohol

Are there any others you want to add? _____

Which ones would you like to talk about now? _____

_____

_____

_____

_____

Ask your parents to tell you how things have changed since the time when they

were growing up: _____

_____

_____

_____

_____

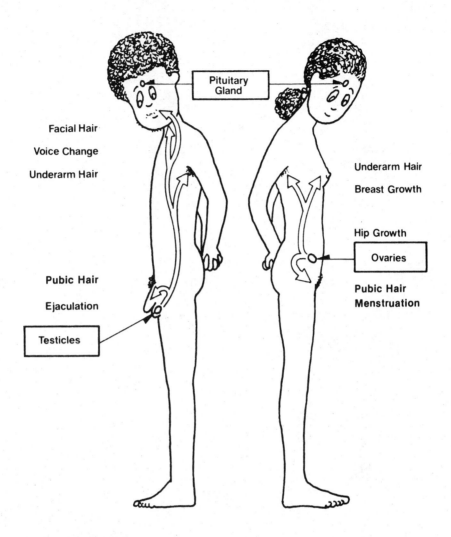

Pituitary Gland

Facial Hair

Voice Change

Underarm Hair

Underarm Hair

Breast Growth

Hip Growth

Ovaries

Pubic Hair

Ejaculation

Pubic Hair
Menstruation

Testicles

THE INSIDE STORY

Puberty begins when your body starts to produce more of certain hormones. A **hormone** is a special chemical which is made in a gland and released into the bloodstream. Hormones carry messages from one part of your body to another. Most of the hormones that start puberty come from a gland near the brain, the **pituitary.** These pituitary hormones tell the sex glands that it is time to start making some changes. So the sex glands start making their own hormones, the sex hormones. Female hormones are made in the ovaries, and male hormones are made in the testicles. These male and female hormones cause the changes that are all part of puberty.

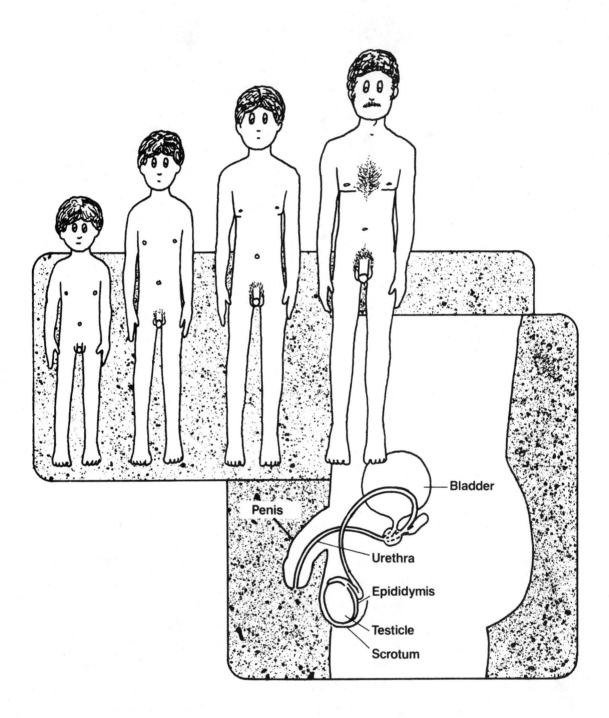

Bladder

Penis

Urethra

Epididymis

Testicle

Scrotum

GROWING UP MALE

On the outside of his body a male has a **penis** and a **scrotum.** The penis is the part of a male's body which is most sensitive to sexual feelings. The scrotum is a thick pouch of skin that holds and protects the testicles. There is a narrow opening through the penis, called the **urethra,** that urine and sperm travel through when they leave the body.

During puberty these parts grow a little larger and more sensitive. Many boys worry that their penis looks different from others. As a matter of fact, penises come in different sizes and shapes, just like feet, ears, and noses. One size and shape is as good as another.

All baby boys are born with a fold of skin, called the **foreskin,** partially covering the glans (tip) of the penis. Some parents have a doctor remove the covering right after birth, by a simple operation called **circumcision.** Other parents don't have it removed. Either way is fine. The only difference is this: males who have a foreskin should clean inside it when they shower or bathe.

During puberty a very important change takes place inside a boy's body: sperm cells start to be made. These cells are extremely tiny. . . seen under a microscope they look like skinny tadpoles. It's these sperm cells that can cause a pregnancy. Every person ever born was started by a male's sperm cell joining with a female's egg cell.

Young sperm cells are made in the **testes,** or **testicles** (both words mean the same thing), two oval-shaped glands inside the scrotum. After they mature the sperm cells move through two very narrow tubes, past glands located just above the scrotum. Here, other fluids are added, making a mixture known as **semen.**

Before we go any further, you should know about something that teenage males experience pretty often: erections. An **erection** happens when extra blood fills spongy tissues inside the penis. The penis becomes larger and firmer, and sticks out from the body. (In spite of what some people say, there is no bone in the penis.)

When a male has an erection it is possible for semen to leave his body. **Ejaculation** is the way semen is released through his penis. This happens when muscles all around his sex organs contract several times, pushing the semen out through the urethra in a few little spurts. At the same time, he usually has a special tingly feeling called **orgasm,** and his whole body feels really good. Of course, a male does not ejaculate every time he has an erection. (A drop or two of fluid may come out, though.) Whether he ejaculates or not, the erection will gradually go away.

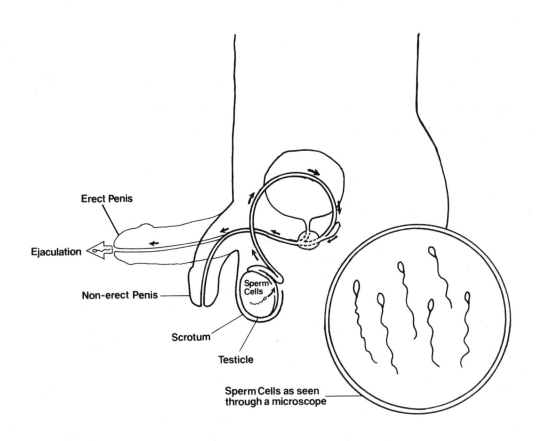

Erect Penis

Ejaculation

Non-erect Penis

Sperm Cells

Scrotum

Testicle

Sperm Cells as seen through a microscope

All kinds of sights, sounds, and thoughts can cause an erection -- even some that don't seem to have anything to do with sex. That's why erections can happen at unexpected times and places, like in math class or while watching TV. Almost all males have erections off and on while they're asleep, and many wake up with an erection.

With each ejaculation, up to a teaspoon of semen is released. Surprisingly, this small amount of fluid contains an average of 400 million sperm cells. Even though semen and urine come out through the same opening in the penis, they are entirely different. Urine and semen cannot be released at the same time. When the penis is fully erect the opening from the bladder closes, so no urine can come out. Ejaculation can be caused in several ways. Many boys have their first ejaculation while they are asleep. This is called a **wet dream**. They may remember having a dream about sex. Other times they won't remember any dream -- there may just be a little spot on the sheet in the morning. This might be a little embarrassing, but most parents know that a wet dream is normal. It has nothing to do with accidentally wetting the bed. A wet dream is a healthy sign of growing up.

Another way boys may ejaculate is through **masturbation**. When a male masturbates, he strokes or rubs his penis in a way that feels good. Masturbation doesn't cause any physical or mental harm. Don't believe stories that it causes boys to run out of semen or lose interest in girls.

In fact, quite a few people believe masturbation is a normal, healthy thing to do. Others just don't feel comfortable about it. They're not sure why -- maybe because of something they were once told. And some people believe it is wrong for religious or moral reasons. But most people -- young, old, married or unmarried -- masturbate from time to time. And they all should know that it won't do them any harm, whether they choose to do it or not.

Males may also ejaculate when they have sexual contact with another person. One kind of contact is often called "petting." This means touching or being touched on the sexually sensitive parts of the body. Ejaculation can happen even without touching the penis directly. Another kind of contact is sexual intercourse. We will say more about intercourse later.

GROWING UP FEMALE

You may have noticed that for many girls puberty starts a year or two earlier than for boys of the same age. One of the first changes is in a girl's breasts. Usually the nipple area gets darker and larger first. Then the fatty tissue that forms the breast begins to grow.

A lot of girls worry about the way their breasts look. Is one a little larger than the other? Are they too big? Too small? The wrong shape? It's easy to get the idea, from TV and movies and magazines, that one "perfect" figure is best for all women. Not true! Beautiful people come in all sizes and shapes. People who learn to appreciate their own special look have a happy self-confidence which makes them likeable and attractive to others.

During puberty, a girl's hips grow wider, too. This makes her waist look smaller, giving her the curved body shape that most mature women have. Like breasts, some girls' hips grow a lot, and others grow just a little.

There are some other small changes which are not so easy to see, even though they are on the outside of the body. These changes are in the **vulva,** a word that means all the sexual parts located between a girl's legs. During puberty all the parts of the vulva grow slightly larger and more sensitive.

The outer part of the vulva -- the **outer labia** or outer **lips** -- is a protective covering for the rest. During puberty, hair grows on and around these outer lips. When the legs are apart, the outer lips separate so that the other parts of the vulva are uncovered. The inner labia, or inner lips, provide another protective layer. Partly hidden by the inner lips, where they join at the top, is the **clitoris.** It is often covered by a little hood of skin, so only a small part can be seen. Like any body part, the clitoris comes in different sizes and shapes, but is usually no larger than a pea. The clitoris is the special part of the female's body which is most sensitive to sexual feelings and touching. It gets slightly larger and firmer when a girl or woman feels sexually excited. In some ways, then, a female's clitoris is like a male's penis.

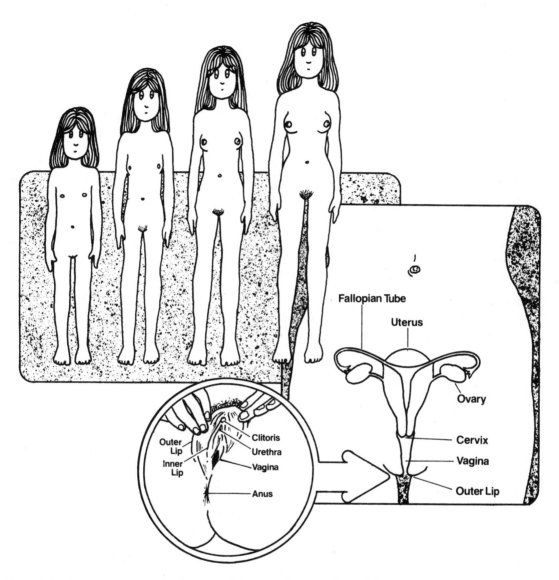

Fallopian Tube

Uterus

Ovary

Cervix

Vagina

Outer Lip

Outer Lip

Inner Lip

Clitoris

Urethra

Vagina

Anus

If a girl or woman masturbates, she usually strokes this very sensitive area. She may also touch other parts of the vulva in a way that feels good. She may sometimes continue until she has an **orgasm**, the special tingly feeling of pleasure that both males and females can have. For a female, as for a male, masturbation does not cause any physical or mental harm. While some people believe it is morally wrong, others believe it is a good way for a girl to learn about her body and how it responds. Many females of all ages masturbate; others choose not to. Either way is normal.

Below the clitoris is the tiny opening of the **urethra.** As in a male, this opening is used for urinating. Below the urethra a female has a larger opening, called the **vagina**, which connects with the inside reproductive organs. Many girls have a thin ring of skin at the opening of the vagina, called the **hymen.** The hymen is small and hidden in the vaginal opening, so it cannot be seen in the drawing. Though it is just a partial covering, it may provide a little extra protection. An adult woman rarely has a complete hymen, because it usually has been stretched to the sides of the vaginal opening. This may happen during exercise, medical examinations, or while using tampons. If not, it will happen when she first has sexual intercourse. So you can see that a girl's hymen may be gone even though she has never had sexual intercourse.

Another opening located near the vulva is the **anus.** This is the opening for bowel movements, so, of course, males have this opening, too. While both males and females have a urethra and an anus, females also have a third opening, the vagina. This is the opening for sexual intercourse, childbirth, and menstruation.

MENSTRUATION

A very important part of a girl's puberty is her first menstrual period. Menstruation, or "having a period," is a sign that her body is maturing, and she is becoming able to get pregnant.

Pregnancy is possible when an **ovum** (egg cell) is ripened and released from one of her **ovaries**. This happens about once a month, and is called **ovulation.** The ovum is very tiny -- smaller than the head of a pin. After it leaves the ovary, the ovum moves down the **Fallopian tube**.

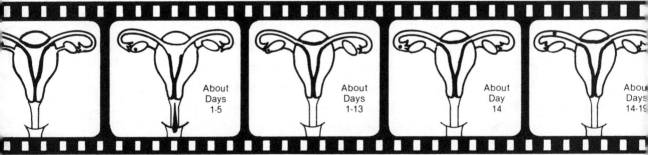

Menstruation–Lining Shed   Ovum Matures   Ovulation–Ovum Released   ...Moves Through Tube

About Days 1-5   About Days 1-13   About Day 14   About Days 14-19

If a male's sperm cell reaches the Fallopian tube at this time, it will probably join with the ovum. This joining of egg and sperm is called **fertilization.** After the egg is fertilized, it continues moving through the tube, until it reaches the uterus. The **uterus**, also called the "womb", is an organ that every female has low in her abdomen (tummy). The uterus has a special lining, rich in blood and nutrients. There, the fertilized egg can attach and grow. That is how pregnancy begins.

If the egg is **not** fertilized by a sperm, there is no pregnancy and the egg dissolves. The special lining of the uterus is no longer needed, so it breaks down and leaves the body. For about 3 to 7 days this menstrual fluid, made up of the blood-rich lining, comes out through the vagina. This is called **menstruation.**

A mature female menstruates about once each month. The average time, from the beginning of one menstrual period to the beginning of the next one, is 28 days. But it can range from 20 to 40 days for different women. When girls first start having periods, they sometimes skip a month, or even a few months, at a time. As they get older, most have their periods more regularly. But even adult women sometimes have late periods. Some things that can make a period late are:

emotional stress	major changes in diet
great excitement	traveling or change in climate
sickness	loss of sleep

A woman usually has no periods while she is pregnant. Otherwise, menstruation usually occurs regularly until a woman is about 50 years old. Then she will gradually stop having periods and will no longer be able to get pregnant.

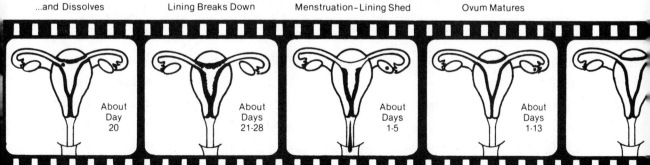

...and Dissolves   Lining Breaks Down   Menstruation–Lining Shed   Ovum Matures

About Day 20   About Days 21-28   About Days 1-5   About Days 1-13

MORE ABOUT MENSTRUATION

To absorb the menstrual fluid, girls and women use either pads (sanitary napkins) or tampons. Both are made of absorbent materials, and are changed several times a day. They are sold in any drug store or supermarket.

Pads cover the opening of the vagina. Most kinds are held in place by an adhesive strip that sticks to the underwear, or by a special belt. Tampons are worn inside the vagina. Many girls and women find them more convenient than pads. The muscles of the vagina hold them in place so they cannot fall out. And since the vagina is only a few inches long and ends at the uterus, a tampon cannot possibly be lost inside the body.

Deciding whether to use pads or tampons is a personal choice. Both come in a variety of types and sizes. Many women use pads sometimes and tampons at other times. Girls might want to try several different products to find the ones they like best.

One word of caution: a disease called toxic shock syndrome (TSS) occurs most often among girls and women who use tampons. Although TSS is not yet fully understood, there are ways a girl or woman can protect herself from getting it. To be on the safe side, tampons should be changed at least once every six hours, and a pad should be worn, instead, for at least a few hours of each day during menstrual periods.

Girls who want to read more about taking care of themselves during menstruation can read one of the pamphlets or books listed at the end of this book.

Many girls feel glad when their periods first start, because this means that their bodies are growing and working normally. Others may at first feel that having periods is a "drag." Some people even act like menstruation is dirty or shameful, maybe because they do not understand it. While menstruating may sometimes seem inconvenient, it is a special womanly sign of a healthy body.

Most women feel fine during their periods. Some have a little discomfort during or just before. Cramping in the lower back or abdomen, slight weight gain, a feeling of heaviness, headaches, or feeling edgy and easily upset are common symptoms. Many girls have these problems less and less as they get older. A healthy diet and regular exercise may help, but if discomfort is really severe, a girl should see her doctor.

During puberty a girl may notice another change in her body. There may be a little bit of clear or whitish fluid in or around the vagina, or on her underwear. This normal discharge is the vagina's way of keeping clean, just as tears and saliva naturally keep the eyes and mouth clean. A small amount of fluid is always present in the vagina. A girl or woman may notice more moisture at certain times, especially around the time of ovulation, about a week after a menstrual period ends. Daydreams, night dreams, and exciting thoughts, as well as masturbation and sexual contact, can also cause extra wetness. If there is no itching, burning or other discomfort there is no need to worry. All this is perfectly normal.

THE PUBERTY PUZZLE

All the answers to this crossword puzzle come from the parts of this book that you have just read. Fill in the answers you know, and ask your parents for help with the ones you're not sure about. The correct answers are shown below.

Across

3. The male sex cell which can fertilize an ovum is called a _____ cell.
6. When a male's penis becomes larger and firmer, this is an _____.
7. The _____ produce female hormones and store egg cells.
8. The _____ produce sperm cells and the male hormone.
10. An _____ is released from the ovary about once a month in mature females.
12. The female organ that is most sensitive to sexual feelings is the _____.
13. _____ are produced in the sex glands of both males and females and cause the changes of puberty.

Down

1. A fertilized ovum (egg) attaches and grows in a woman's _____.
2. The male organ that can become erect is the _____.
4. About once a month the lining of the uterus breaks down and leaves the body. This is called _____.
5. The opening where this menstrual fluid comes out of the body is the _____.
9. The _____ is the thick pouch of skin that holds a male's testicles.
11. _____ is the special tingly feeling of sexual pleasure in both men and women.

SEXUAL INTERCOURSE

Now that you know about the bodies of both sexes, you can understand what sexual intercourse is. From the illustrations you can see that the male and female sex organs are shaped so that they can fit together. This makes it possible for a man and a woman to have sexual intercourse.

When a man and woman are attracted to each other, being close and touching can make them feel sexually excited. This means they have good feelings all over, the woman's vagina becomes more moist, and the man's penis becomes erect. When they feel this way, they may want to be still closer. If they decide to have sexual intercourse, they put their bodies close together, so that the man's penis can slide into the woman's vagina. This pleases them both, and they continue moving in ways that feel good. They enjoy being as close as two people can be. Intercourse may last just a minute or two, or for quite a while, often until one or both has an orgasm. Usually the man ejaculates and his erection gradually goes away. After intercourse many couples continue to hold each other for a while, and enjoy feeling close.

These intimate feelings are one reason why sexual intercourse is so important. Another reason is that *sexual intercourse is how pregnancies get started.* When the male ejaculates, sperm cells are released in the female's vagina, and move toward her Fallopian tubes. If an egg cell is there at the time, it will probably be fertilized and a pregnancy could begin.

In the right circumstances, sexual intercourse can be one of the most rewarding experiences a couple can have together. But it is not a simple matter, and you will find it easier to understand when you are grown up. For most people, having intercourse is very personal, and belongs only in a close, trusting, mature relationship.

Some people have intercourse while they are still in their early teens. Most wait until they are older. For many reasons it's smarter to wait. For one thing, some teenagers aren't ready and end up feeling hurt or upset. Also, having intercourse can create serious problems a young person isn't ready to deal with, like pregnancy and sexually transmitted infection (STI).

This book will tell you more about pregnancy and STIs. For now, just remember that anyone who has sexual intercourse needs to know how to prevent them. Some teenagers don't believe these problems can happen to them. But they can—even the first time a person has intercourse.

There are other good reasons for teenagers to wait before they have intercourse. Why is it better to wait? Together with your parents, try listing some advantages here:

_____

_____

_____

_____

_____

PREGNANCY

So, pregnancy is started by sexual intercourse. Now we will tell you about what happens between the time when the egg and sperm are joined and the time a baby is born.

Fertilization happens in one of the Fallopian tubes, at the end closest to the ovary. For the next 4 or 5 days, the fertilized egg cell continues to move down the tube until it reaches the uterus. This is where most of its growth will take place.

By the time the fertilized egg reaches the uterus, the blood-rich lining is ready to give it the nourishment it needs for growing. Within a few days, it attaches to the inside of the uterus **(implantation)**. Here, it grows for about 9 months. Until the end of the second month it is called an **embryo.** From then until birth, it is called a **fetus.**

As the pregnancy develops, some remarkable changes happen. From the place inside the uterus where the egg is attached, the **umbilical cord** grows. This cord carries nourishment and oxygen, both needed for growth, from the woman's bloodstream to the bloodstream of the developing fetus. Since the fetus does not eat or breathe until it is born, everything it needs must pass through this cord. Also, the **amniotic sac,** a bag filled with watery fluid, grows around the embryo, and stays there throughout the pregnancy. This "bag of water" cushions and protects the developing fetus.

Of course, to make room for the growing fetus, the uterus must stretch a lot. During pregnancy, the uterus changes from the size of a pear to the size of a small watermelon. Naturally, the pregnant woman's shape also changes to make room for her growing uterus. After the baby is born, the uterus gradually shrinks back to the size it was before pregnancy.

Does your mom have a picture she can show you of herself while she was pregnant?

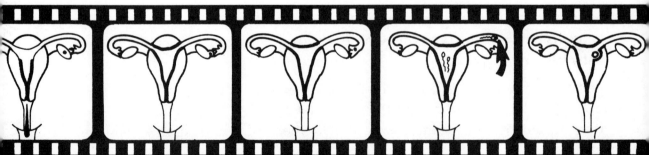

Menstruation
–Lining Shed

Ovum Matures

Ovulation–Ovum Released

Fertilization
–Ovum Joined By Sperm

Implantation
–Pregnancy Begins

CHILDBIRTH

After about nine months of pregnancy, the mother gives birth to her baby. With each passing month, the fetus has come closer to being ready for birth and able to survive outside its mother's body. When the time for birth is near, the mother feels the muscles of her uterus firmly squeezing every few minutes. As the squeezing gets stronger, the **cervix** (the opening at the bottom of the uterus) gradually stretches open more and more. This may take many hours. During this time, the mother needs only to relax and patiently wait, as the muscles of her uterus work harder and harder. Finally, the cervix stretches open wide enough for the baby's head to pass through. Then the mother begins to push down, as hard as she can, with the muscles of her abdomen. Her effort combines with the squeezing of her uterus to push the baby into the vagina, usually head first. Then within minutes, the new baby slips from the mother's body into the outside world.

When a baby comes out, it is still attached to its umbilical cord. Now that it can start breathing and eating, it doesn't need this connection any more. Soon after birth, the cord is cut, close to the baby's tummy. Cutting the cord is painless, and the small cut will soon heal. What remains becomes the **navel**, or belly button. Everybody has a navel where their umbilical cord used to be.

| 3 Month Fetus | 6 Month Fetus | 9 Month Fetus | Childbirth Begins | Menstrual Cycle Returns |

Is there anything you would like to ask your mom or dad about your own birth? You can write your questions, and their answers, here:

_____

_____

_____

_____

_____

_____

Childbirth usually takes place the way we have described, but occasionally something unusual happens. If you are interested in some of the unusual things, you and your parents might want to do some reading in a good book or encyclopedia. Some interesting things to learn about are: twins, triplets, Caesarean section, breech birth, and premature birth.

While a woman is pregnant, her breasts get ready to make milk for feeding the baby after it is born. Around the time of birth, they begin to produce this milk. Most babies are able to suck milk from their mother's breasts soon after birth, and many mothers enjoy feeding their babies this way. They know that their breast milk is a complete nourishing food for a new baby. Of course, for one reason or another, a mother may prefer to feed her baby with a bottle. Either way is fine.

Which way were you fed when you were an infant? _____

How long did you drink milk before you started eating other foods? _____

_____

HEREDITY

What makes one person tall and another short? Why do some people in the same family look alike, and others look different? Why do identical twins look alike? Why do dogs give birth to little dogs, and cows have little cows, and humans have little humans?

Inside every cell of every living thing are many **chromosomes.** These chromosomes carry the master plan for how that plant or animal will grow. The shape of your nose, the color of your skin, and the type of hair you have are all controlled by your own individual set of chromosomes.

All humans get half of their chromosomes from the father's sperm and half from the mother's ovum. Since a child only gets half of each parent's master plan, some parts are included and some are left out. That is why most children look something like their parents, but not exactly like them.

Every man has some sperm cells that carry a "female" chromosome and others that carry a "male" chromosome. Whether a new baby is a girl or a boy depends on which type of sperm fertilized the mother's ovum.

WHY DO PEOPLE HAVE SEX?

So now you know quite a bit about puberty. You know that puberty means your body will change to an adult body, capable of reproducing. You know that all through life everyone has sexual feelings and that these feelings grow stronger during puberty. Sexual feelings are an important part of life, and also a very personal part. Most of the time we choose to keep our sexual thoughts and feelings to ourselves.

It may seem strange to you that people sometimes share their sexual feelings with another person. Sexual intercourse, especially, may seem hard to understand. You may wonder, "Why would anyone do **that**? . . . Why is 'having sex' such a big deal?". The answer is that sexual intercourse can add a lot of happiness to a person's life, or it can cause **big** problems. That's why it **is** a big deal. That's why it may seem that everyone is interested in it, or worried about it.

The better we understand sex, the better we are able to make responsible decisions about it. Then it can bring happiness, and not problems, to ourselves and to others.

MAKING BABIES

All living things reproduce their kind, and humans do this by having sexual intercourse. If we did not, the human race would not last long.

When a woman and man decide to make a baby, though, they are not usually thinking about the whole human race. They are looking forward to the joy of having and raising a child. Parenthood is a lifelong opportunity to love and care for another human being. It is also a lifelong responsibility. That's why deciding to make a baby is one of the most important decisions a person can make. Everyone who decides to have sexual intercourse needs to think very carefully about the possibility that a pregnancy could start.

Often a couple decides to have intercourse even if they do not want a baby right then. Some people prefer to have no children. Some prefer to wait until a time when they can better care for a child. Some already have the number of children they want. These couples use some kind of birth control **(contraception).** By using contraception, a couple can have intercourse and be reasonably sure they will not start a pregnancy.

One kind of birth control you probably have heard about is the contraceptive pill (or just "the pill"). You might also have heard of condoms ("rubbers"). There are several other ways to prevent pregnancy, each with its own advantages. One way or another, they all work by preventing the egg and sperm from getting together and growing in the uterus. Some methods are prescribed by doctors or clinics, and some are sold in drugstores without a prescription. If you want to find out more about different methods of contraception, see the reading list for some suggested books.

Being a good parent is one of the toughest jobs in the world. It takes a lot to be ready for parenthood. Try listing the five most important qualities you think a good parent needs to have, and ask your mom or dad to do the same:

Your List:

_____

_____

_____

_____

_____

Your Parent's List:

_____

_____

_____

_____

_____

"MAKING LOVE" (without making mistakes)

Though making babies is important, it's not the main reason why couples have sexual intercourse. When two people care very much about each other, intercourse is one of the ways they can share their loving feelings. Joining their bodies in this way gives them a special kind of pleasure. We call this "making love."

Even though intercourse can give this unique pleasure, it's not as simple as it may sound. Many teenagers face a lot of pressure to have intercourse before they are ready. Sometimes it seems like everybody else is doing it. It's easy to get this idea from TV shows, movies, and big-talking friends.

But the truth is, most teenagers are not having sex. Most TV shows and movies use sex for one simple reason: it gets attention and makes money. But these shows rarely show life as it really is. And friends who try to get you to have sex are not thinking about what's best for **you.**

There are some important things that TV, movies, and friends usually leave out. For one thing, making love involves our most intimate feelings. Being this close with someone before you are ready can leave you feeling embarrassed, hurt, or used. Adding sex can make a nice relationship complicated and difficult.

For another, anyone who has sex needs to know how to avoid getting a sexually transmitted infection (STI). The most serious STI is AIDS, a disease caused by a virus (the human immunodeficiency virus, or "HIV"). AIDS keeps the body from being able to fight off other diseases. Nearly everyone with AIDS gets sicker and weaker and eventually dies. Sex is one of the ways that people get HIV. Some other ways are sharing needles to shoot drugs, and during childbirth if the mother is infected.

There are many other STIs, too. Some common ones are chlamydia, herpes, genital warts, and gonorrhea. Each one causes different problems, such as sores or damage to internal organs. Like HIV, other STIs are passed from person to person when they have sex.

But a person may be infected without showing any signs of the disease for weeks, months, or even years. This makes it much easier for these diseases to spread, because people often have the germs without knowing it. The only way to be sure is to go to a doctor or clinic for testing. There are treatments for all STIs, so anyone who might have one should be checked as soon as possible.

Of course, the best thing is to protect yourself from getting an STI in the first place. There are several ways to do this. One way is not having sex: STIs can only be caught through close contact with someone who is already infected. As long as you don't have sex, you won't get a sexually transmitted disease.

Someday, though, you will probably want to have a relationship that includes sex. When you are mature and ready for this, you can protect yourself by having "safer sex." Safer sex means using a condom and a germ-killing chemical. It also means being as certain as you can that the person you have sex with is not infected. You will need to talk with that person about all this, and you will need to trust that person.

What kind of person do you imagine would have an STI? In fact, **all** kinds of people get them. You can't tell by people's clothes, or who their friends are, or where they live. You can only tell by knowing someone very well, talking about STIs, and trusting that person to know about STIs and to be honest with you.

You can see there are lots of things you need to know before you're ready for sex. Learning about STIs and safer sex is one part. Learning about birth control is another. You also need to understand yourself. And you need to be able to be a good partner. That's a lot to learn, but you have plenty of time. Don't let anyone push you before you're good and ready.

What else would you like to know about STIs? Birth control? Safer sex? _____

_____

_____

_____

How do you know when you can trust someone? See if your parents can help you figure this out: _____

_____

_____

MAKING SENSE...OF LOVE AND SEX

Though having intercourse is often called "making love," love and sex are not the same thing. "Love" is a word that people use to mean many things. We love our parents, and we love our pets. We love our close friends, and we love our grandparents. You might have even heard someone say "I love chocolate ice cream!" In each case the feelings are a little different.

And then of course there's "falling in love." When two people "fall in love" with each other, they want to be together a lot and want to share personal thoughts and feelings. They really care about each other's feelings, and they both feel good about themselves most of the time they are together.

In time, the excitement of falling in love may change to a deep feeling of love and trust for each other. Two people who share this kind of love usually want their relationship to last for a long time. They plan to work things out together. Whether times are good or times are tough, they know they can count on each other. For a couple like this, sex can be a way of expressing their loving feelings. Most people think this is the best kind of sexual relationship, and the best kind of marriage.

But the fact is, love and sex don't always go together. Many people love each other without having sex, and others have sex without love. Some people have sex just for the physical pleasure they get from it. Others believe this is wrong, or just feel sure they would not enjoy sex without love. To avoid problems everyone needs to remember that:

—no one has to have sex just to please someone else

—having sex will not make love happen

—it is mean to let someone think you love him or her when you really don't.

Of course, many people fall in love before they are ready for sex or for marriage. So it's a good thing that sex is not the only way to show these feelings. Other things, like communication and really caring about one another, are more important in a loving relationship.

There are many ways, besides sex, to express feelings of love and closeness to someone. Doing special favors for him or her, being a good listener, holding hands, giving flowers...these are just a few ways. Can you and your mom or dad think of some other ways of showing love? Try making a list: _____

_____

_____

How do the people in your family show love to each other? _____

_____

_____

Which of these ways would also be good ways of showing love to a boyfriend or girlfriend? _____

_____

_____

A GOOD START

So now you know more about puberty. You can see it has a lot to do with sex and reproduction. These are big subjects, and there are a lot of other interesting things to know. By sharing this book, you and your parents have made a good start. But any book covers only a small part of all there is to know. Hopefully you will continue to talk and learn together.

There may be other things you are wondering about. If there are, list them here:

_____

_____

Ask your parents if there are other things which they would like you to know, now that you are almost a teenager, and write their answers here: _____

_____

_____

During the next few years you will learn a lot more about understanding yourself and others. From each new person you get to know, you will learn more and more about what you want from a close relationship. No one knows this ahead of time. Learning about love and sex continues all through life.

For Further Reading . . .

MORE GOOD BOOKS FOR YOU
AND YOUR PARENTS

The Family Book About Sexuality
by Mary S. Calderone, M.D. and Eric W. Johnson (HarperCollins, 1990).

A general family reference book. Covers sexuality and its role in people's lives from childhood through puberty, adulthood, and old age. Includes basic information on sexual development along with special sections on reproduction, love and marriage, disabilities, sexually transmitted infections, and many other topics, as well as a 50-page "encyclopedia" section. 304 pages.

Period
by Ann Gardner-Loulan, Bonnie Lopez, and Marcia Quackenbush (Volcano Press, 1991).

For pre-teen girls, a book about menstruation, feelings about it and taking care of it. Charming illustrations and personal stories add humor to the topic. Includes a removable parents' guide. Also available in Spanish. 98 pages.

The "What's Happening to My Body?" Book for Girls and
The "What's Happening to My Body?" Book for Boys
by Lynda Madaras (Newmarket Press, 1988).

For nine- to fifteen-year-olds and their parents. Provides detailed information on the physical changes of puberty for boys and for girls, and each book includes a chapter on the changes experienced by the opposite sex. Age-appropriate information on AIDS and other sexually transmitted infections, pregnancy, childbirth, and birth control as well as a chapter on "Romantic and Sexual Feelings." 250+ pages.

Changing Bodies, Changing Lives: A Book for Teens on Sex and Relationships
by Ruth Bell (Random House, 1988).

For fifteen- to nineteen-year-olds, a book which covers many adolescent concerns about puberty, sex, relationships, emotional and physical health. Presents many points of view through quotes from teenagers themselves. Deals with relationships between teens and parents, teens and peers, and sex-role expectations. Special sections on menstruation, birth control, teen pregnancy, and mental health. 254 pages.

PAMPHLETS
may be available at your local Planned Parenthood,®
or order single copies at $1.00, including postage, from the address given for each title

"Daddy, Can You Tell Me?" Helping Your Young Child Learn About Sexuality.
(Planned Parenthood® of Central California, 255 N. Fulton, Fresno, CA 93701) Tips for fathers who want to help their kids learn about sex from a responsible male's point of view, and not leave it to the streets, the soap operas, or only to mom. 10 pages.

Feeling Good About Growing Up. (Planned Parenthood® Federation of America (PPFA), 810 Seventh Avenue, New York, NY 10019) To help teens and pre-teens feel good about growing up. Basic information in simple, direct and reassuring language. 24 pages.

Kids and AIDS: A Guide for Parents. (PPFA, see above) Designed to help parents discuss this difficult subject with toddlers through teens, including "Ten Basic Facts Kids Need to Know" and "Six Gifts of Self-Protection" a parent should give to a child. 20 pages.

How to Talk with Your Child About Sexuality: A Parent's Guide. (PPFA, see above) Help with preparing for and answering the questions of pre-schoolers to adolescents about sex and sexuality. 12 pages.

How to Talk with Your Teen About the Facts of Life. (PPFA, see above) For parents of teens and pre-teens, the facts they need to discuss reproduction, masturbation, menstruation, pregnancy, birth control and sexually transmitted infections, with attractive illustrations to make discussions easier.

ORDER FORM

FOR ADDITIONAL COPIES OF **LET'S TALK ABOUT...S-E-X, Revised Edition**
(or the Spanish/English bilingual version, HABLEMOS ACERCA DEL...S-E-X-O)

contact your local bookstore or: Planned Parenthood of Central California
Publications
255 N. Fulton
Fresno, CA 93701-1600
(209) 488-4917

Please send:

_____ copies of LET'S TALK ABOUT...S-E-X @ $5.95 each = _____

_____ copies of HABLEMOS ACERCA DEL...S-E-X-O @ $4.95 each = _____

Sales tax: Please add 7.75% for books shipped to California addresses _____

Shipping: Add $2.00 for the first book and 50 cents for each additional book _____

All orders must be prepaid. Make checks or money orders
payable to Planned Parenthood of Central California (PPCC).

TOTAL ENCLOSED _____

To:

Name/Organization _____

Address _____

City _____ State _____ Zip _____

Telephone (   ) _____

Agencies and organizations may qualify for special discounts on quantity purchases of
these titles. For further information, please write or phone PPCC at the address above.

ORDER FORM

FOR ADDITIONAL COPIES OF **LET'S TALK ABOUT...S-E-X, Revised Edition**
(or the Spanish/English bilingual version, HABLEMOS ACERCA DEL...S-E-X-O)

contact your local bookstore or: Planned Parenthood of Central California
Publications
255 N. Fulton
Fresno, CA 93701-1600
(209) 488-4917

Please send:

_____ copies of LET'S TALK ABOUT...S-E-X @ $5.95 each = _____

_____ copies of HABLEMOS ACERCA DEL...S-E-X-O @ $4.95 each = _____

Sales tax: Please add 7.75% for books shipped to California addresses _____

Shipping: Add $2.00 for the first book and 50 cents for each additional book _____

All orders must be prepaid. Make checks or money orders
payable to Planned Parenthood of Central California (PPCC).

TOTAL ENCLOSED _____

To:

Name/Organization _____

Address _____

City _____ State _____ Zip _____

Telephone (_____) _____

Agencies and organizations may qualify for special discounts on quantity purchases of
these titles. For further information, please write or phone PPCC at the address above.